IMAGES OF SCOTLAND

MARITIME
ABERDEEN

Aberdeen Trawler. The Trial Trip.

IMAGES OF SCOTLAND

MARITIME ABERDEEN

JOHN EDWARDS

TEMPUS

Frontispiece: The first trip of the new Aberdeen trawler *Aboyne*.

First published 2004

Tempus Publishing Limited
The Mill, Brimscombe Port,
Stroud, Gloucestershire, GL5 2QG
www.tempus-publishing.com

British Library Cataloguing in Publication Data.
A catalogue record for this book is available from the British Library.

ISBN 0 7524 3218 4

Typesetting and origination by Tempus Publishing Limited.
Printed in Great Britain.

Contents

Acknowledgements

All of the photographs, paintings and plans reproduced in this book are from the Aberdeen Art Gallery and Museums collections and in most instances are maintained by the Aberdeen Maritime Museum.

The vast majority of the collections have been built up over many decades through the generosity of Aberdonians and those closely connected with the city's maritime history. In the case of the wonderful paintings that are reproduced here, many were donated to the museum and, in some instances, purchased with the assistance of grants and bequests.

I wish to acknowledge specifically William Buchan, Tony Clayden, George Leiper and Jim Wood for allowing their pictures to be used in this book.

My thanks go to colleagues who assisted with the typescript and with information, specifically Lyn Gray and Catherine Walker.

Introduction

Aberdeen has been at the centre of maritime industry and events in the United Kingdom for centuries. This most northerly of cities has been in its day the home of the first and finest of British clipper ships, the biggest Scottish fishing port and capital of the European offshore oil and gas industry. Although disadvantaged by its relative remoteness from the rest of the UK, the city has always looked to the sea for its livelihood, trade and sustenance.

With the sea being the prime means of communication since medieval times, Aberdeen took naturally to trade links both to domestic harbours in Scotland and English ports, but also across the North Sea to the Low Countries and the Baltic. These connections fostered a healthy growth in the fishing industry while shipbuilding and trade prospered as engineers steadily transformed the slow moving River Dee Estuary into a complex of quays and docks.

Until the early 1840s the only means of documenting the port, its ships and mariners was through paintings, drawings and maps. Fortunately a rich tradition of commissioning and collecting marine art, ship portraits and harbour plans runs strong in Aberdeen. The legacy of several centuries of collecting such art and documents has been passed to the Aberdeen Art Gallery and Museums Collections, as well as local and university libraries and archives. The Aberdeen Maritime Museum maintains a fine collection of 'Captains' Portraits' of ships, as well as pictures of the city from the eighteenth century, providing us with a unique view of a dynamic maritime city. These paintings record the age of sail and can be regarded as accurate documents of the harbour and its ships. Each was likely to have been commissioned by a ship owner, captain or merchant who would insist on a complete and accurate rendering of their prize vessel.

Thanks to the coming of photography we are in the fortunate position of having both paintings and photographs of vessels and the harbour available to compare with and complement each other. In this way we can often pick out details on the ships in one medium that cannot be seen in the other. This happy period of overlap has lasted in some instances to the present day, with owners enjoying the tradition of producing a ship portrait as well as an extensive photographic archive of the new ship.

Again, the Aberdeen Maritime Museum has collected thousands of such photographs covering all the subject areas shown in this book. The earliest views show the early days of shipbuilding with fine wooden clipper ships being constructed on beach slipways. They show the men who designed and built *Thermopylae* and other incredibly fast and reliable clipper ships built for the thrilling China tea races of the 1860s and '70s. As steamships began to trade from the city and eventually provide the means to create a huge mechanised fishing fleet, commercial photographers were there to provide their services to a host of new enterprises.

Aberdeen boomed in the 1880s with the rise of the trawlers and associated fish processors. New industries required more quays and the new engineering works expanded the port, creating improved dockside facilities that speeded up trade and brought increased wealth to the city as a whole. People flocked to Aberdeen to fill the newly created maritime-linked jobs and also the thousands of construction and service industry jobs that these developments had produced.

The trawlers built for fishing were adapted during two world wars to serve as minesweepers and coastal escort vessels. Their extremely sturdy design matched by the strength of the crew meant that the fleet of small Aberdeen ships did their bit to defend the country.

The Museum's photographic collection begins to reflect the increased access to cameras around the 1920s with more and more 'snaps' of friends, family and co-workers appearing. These pictures help to show us the way of life in fishing communities and associated marine trades during the twentieth century, and serve to bring balance to a collection dominated by commercial photography during the previous century. Through these photographs we are able to see Aberdeen's 'Golden Sands', or witness one of the fine North Boats setting sail for a cruise to Norway. We witness wartime ship work and the baiting of fishing lines by grannies and young children. They engage us today because they offer us a view of the past we can relate to through our own family photograph albums.

The oil-boom era is reflected in this volume as we see the nature of shipping in the harbour change from general cargo vessels and trawlers to the massive and incredibly powerful oil supply ships. The industry has been in Aberdeen since the early 1970s and its impact on the look of the harbour and the industries it fosters is apparent in any modern photograph of the port.

The Aberdeen Maritime Museum is like a giant family album reflecting centuries of maritime trades, shipbuilders and seafarers through the medium of pictures. This book selects many images from albums and framed pictures that came from the houses of shipbuilders and merchants, through to scenes of everyday life on the quaysides and ships as seen through the viewfinders of box Brownie cameras. The collection reflects all aspects of the long life of this old port city and principally the work and ingenuity of the people of Aberdeen, who, through their maritime enterprise, developed and sailed some of the finest ships in the world.

one

Age of Sail

Above: An unknown brig at Footdee. This is one of the earliest photographs of the harbour and probably dates from the 1840s. Prominent on the left is the tower of St Clement's Church which was the parish church of the seafarers and shipbuilders. The graveyard is the resting place of shipmasters as well as Alexander Hall, builder of some of Aberdeen's finest clipper ships.

Above: The Duthie family album includes this photograph from around 1870. The unidentified man is very likely one of the famous ship-owners and shipbuilders having on his lap a waterline model of one of the ships of the Duthie fleet.

Opposite below: The Duthie-built *Prince Alfred* on her launch day in 1862. This shows the extent of completion the ship was in prior to launch with the three masts secured by standing rigging. Following launch, a quick fit-out would see the addition of upper masts, spars and running rigging as well as final works on deckhouses and accommodation below decks. The photograph gives a flavour of working shipyard conditions, with building materials and tools freely strewn around the slipway.

Above: The schooner *Kelpie* built by Alexander Hall & Co. for Charles Horsfall & Sons of Liverpool at a cost of £3,000. This early photograph is signed by James Lamb in the year the vessel was built, Aberdeen 1855.

Lastage for
LIVERPOOL

THE FINE NEW CLIPPER SHIP,
"REINDEER,"
CAPTAIN ENWRIGHT,
500 TONS BURTHEN,

Is now on the Berth Loading for the above Port, and will be despatched

ON MONDAY FIRST,
The 4th December,

SATURDAY being the last day for Shipment of Goods.

SPLENDID ACCOMMODATION FOR PASSENGERS.

For Freight or Passage apply to
JOHN COOK,
59, MARISCHAL STREET,

ABERDEEN, November 28, 1848.

J. AVERY, Printer, Crown Court, 43, Union Street.

Above: Original poster seeking cargo for the new clipper ship *Reindeer*, 4 December 1848. The agents for the ship were the well-established Aberdeen firm of John Cook whose offices on Marischal Street were very close to the harbour.

Opposite below: The *Schomberg* was the largest wooden ship ever built in Aberdeen. Shown here in 1855 during its fitting-out alongside the quay adjacent to the Alexander Hall yard, the 248ft long, 2,284-ton ship would soon set sail for Australia. Captain James 'Bully' Forbes would seem to have been obsessed with making a name for himself by driving ship and crew to break the time record. Unfortunately for all concerned, Forbes became famous for entirely the wrong reasons when he navigated the *Schomberg* aground with the total loss of the ship near Melbourne on 26 December 1855.

Above: William Duthie senior in a studio print of 1860. He founded the firm William Duthie & Co. in 1811. His company was responsible for many of the city's finest clipper ships. William Duthie died in October 1861 and is buried in St Clement's churchyard, close to the site of his shipyard.

Opposite above: The *Ann Duthie* pictured at Footdee shortly after completion in 1868. The Duthie house flag, consisting of a hand holding a dagger on a white shield with a blue background, is flying from the ship's main mast. The spire of St Clement's church is visible between the foremast and mainmast while a set of sheerlegs are to the right behind the vessel's elegant bowsprit.

Opposite below: An advertising card for a future sailing of the Duthie-built and owned clipper *Ann Duthie*, 1875. The virtues of the ship and crew are extolled in the record of previous voyages. Captain George Morgan had made his reputation by taking command of the *Rifleman* in 1873, after the murder of Captain Longmuir on the high seas.

The Australian and New Zealand Form of Bill of Lading to be used for all Shipments
by this Vessel; and in cases where the Freight is payable in London,
Cash will be required in exchange for Bills of Lading.

TO FOLLOW
THE
"BRILLIANT."

HAVING
A LARGE PART OF HER CARGO
ENGAGED.

DIRECT FOR

SYDNEY

The magnificent Aberdeen-built Clipper-Ship

ANN DUTHIE, A I 17 YEARS

(Owned by WILLIAM DUTHIE, JUN., ESQ., of Aberdeen.)

G. MORGAN, Commander.

994 Tons Register.   SOUTH WEST INDIA DOCKS.

Previous Passages of this splendid Vessel—

Out to Sydney	72 Days.
Home	74 ,,
Sydney to London	78 ,,

Mate's Receipts for water-borne Goods must be left before Bills of Lading can be signed, and the Brokers
will not be responsible for Demurrage of any Craft sent alongside without their orders.

For Freight or Passage apply to

HOULDER BROTHERS & CO.,

LIVERPOOL OFFICES:—14, WATER STREET   146, LEADENHALL STREET, LONDON, E.C.
GLASGOW 30, HOPE STREET.

Complementing the painting of *Rifleman* (see page 49) is this photograph of the ship alongside Footdee, possibly just after completion in 1860. It is useful to compare the two views, as features of rigging often would not be visible in early photographs due to the long exposure. On the other hand, the artist would work to the owner's instructions and would be required to portray the vessel to his satisfaction with every detail properly shown.

Duthie-built *John Duthie* in Sydney harbour, *c.*1866. Although paintings and photographs exist of the ship off Gibraltar and Australia, none have been found in her home port of Aberdeen. This is not unusual, with even world-famous ships like *Thermopylae* failing to be depicted at Aberdeen's quays, owners and captains apparently preferring the traditional ship's portrait.

Captain George Morgan, *c.*1880. Morgan came to notoriety in 1873 when he had to take command of the Duthie ship *Rifleman,* en route to Australia when its Captain, James Longmuir, was murdered by the steward Wilhelm Krauss. Morgan completed the 110-day voyage, bringing crew, cargo and passengers to the safety of Sydney and Krauss to justice. Captain Morgan received a gold watch from the grateful owners and continued to master Duthie ships in the years that followed the incident.

CAPE OF GOOD HOPE.

The First-class Brig,

"BON-ACCORD"

Is now on the Berth at

WATERLOO QUAY,

For the above Port, and will be despatched towards the end of the present month.

Parties sending out Consignments of Goods, may, especially at present, in consequence of the War, count on highly remunerative returns ; and the Subscriber will give information as to long-established and trustworthy Agents at Cape Town, with whom he has been in communication, and also as to the kinds of Goods most likely to meet a ready sale.

The Vessel is a Fast Sailer, and can take a few Passengers at a moderate rate of fare.

Shippers who formerly sent their Goods to London for Shipment, will make a considerable saving by shipping here.

APPLY TO

JOHN COOK.

48, MARISCHAL STREET,
Aberdeen, April 5, 1851.

GEO. CORNWALL, PRINTER, 34, CASTLE STREET.

A poster for the *Bon-Accord*, 5 April 1851. Several ships have borne the name of the city of Aberdeen's motto, and it would appear that Alexander Hall built this vessel in 1845.

The pride of the Aberdeen White Star Line *Thermopylae* in Sydney harbour during the 1880s. The tea clipper aroused great interest during its design, launch and fit-out, with a record maiden voyage to Australia anticipated. Aberdonians were not disappointed with their ship as it arrived in Sydney after a record eighty-nine days. *Thermopylae* raced in the great tea races of the 1870s and beat the *Cutty Sark* in the famous race of 1872. The ship was later reduced to a barque rig and was a timber carrier for Canadian interests in the 1890s. She ended her days as a Portuguese training ship, being ceremonially sunk off Lisbon in 1907.

The figurehead of the *Abergeldie*, built by the Duthies in 1869. The sailing ship was typical of the Duthie line, measuring 218ft in length, 37ft across the beam and with a depth of 21ft. She was designed for the Australian trade and was in Duthie ownership for twenty years. The ship's portrait can be found on page 40.

Jho-Sho-Maru is a true one-off in Aberdeen's maritime history. It was built for Japan through the auspices of Fraserburgh-born Thomas Blake Glover. Glover positioned himself with the Higo clan during the 1860s civil war, promising to build them a massive gunboat in Aberdeen. Faced with this challenge, Glover commissioned Alexander Hall & Co. to build the ship for £46,032 in 1868 (*Thermopylae* by comparison cost £9,000 a year earlier). It bankrupted the shipyard, as a steam gunship had never been built there before, yet the vessel was a success for the Higo clan as they gained ascendancy in Japan and brought long-term business success to Glover.

The deserted deck of the four-masted iron barque *Port Jackson* belies the activity that was the usual norm on a working sailing ship. All lines, spars and fittings are all in proper order yet indicate the amount of work needed to maintain the ship. A crew of twenty would work the vessel on its voyages that routinely included 12,000 mile trips to Australia. Aberdeen's largest vessel survived until 1917 when she was torpedoed by a U-boat.

The crew of the Aberdeen White Star Line clipper ship *Sophocles*, *c*.1880. The ship's life-ring displays both the Red Ensign and the shipping line's flag with its six-pointed star on a blue and red background. The location of the ship is not known although the crew's attire suggests they may be in Sydney, one of their frequent ports of call.

Aberdeen harbour's steam paddle tug's principal daily task was to tow vessels safely through the narrow navigation channel and over the harbour 'bar' at the entrance. This everyday scene from around 1890 shows an unidentified barque leaving the port bound for the North Sea. Tugs were powerful, manoeuvrable and versatile and were sometimes pressed into lifesaving services as well as proving the worth of powered trawling in the 1880s. Nevertheless, their main role was the mundane but essential task of shepherding ships safely to and from Aberdeen.

two

From Estuary
to Harbour

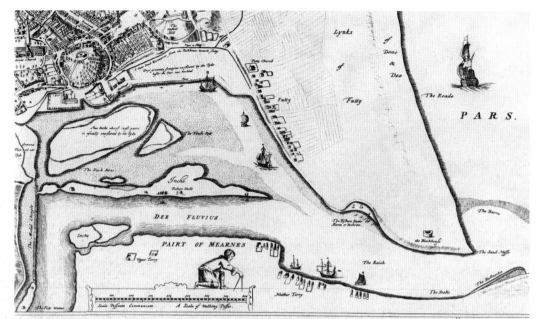

Above: An engraving of the newly completed North Pier, designed by John Smeaton, 1800. The 1,200ft-long pier was built to prevent the blockage of the harbour entrance by sand. The concept was correct but further extensions were required in later years. The newly completed octagonal 'Round House' is seen at the base of the pier with the thriving shipyards of Footdee in the background.

Opposite above: Parson Gordon's map of Aberdeen, drawn in 1661, is the earliest complete plan of the harbour and city. Apart from the quays built on the northern shore of the wide Dee Estuary, little had been done to alter the natural flow of the river. The harbour had many natural obstacles, including rocks and ever shifting sands, making navigation a skilled operation. The map makes clear the connection between the inhabitants of 'New Aberdeen' and the sea, by including the full expanse of the estuary which provided the lifeblood of trade and commerce to the city.

Opposite below: An early engraving of 'New Aberdeen' showing the narrow entrances to the harbour and the channel to the city's main quays, *c.*1692. The sandy 'inches' to the left were the result of the flow of the Dee through this wide estuary. The inches were forever shifting and would be uncovered by each low tide making the area difficult to navigate. The spires of 'Old Aberdeen' are just visible to the right.

This lithograph dating from the 1840s shows a busy port scene from the south. Three fishwives with their baskets and creels are setting off for Aberdeen from Torry in a rowing boat, while a fast sailing ship makes its entrance to the harbour. A sleek clipper-bowed brig is visible in the centre, perhaps paying homage to Aberdeen's growing reputation as the home of fast sailing ships.

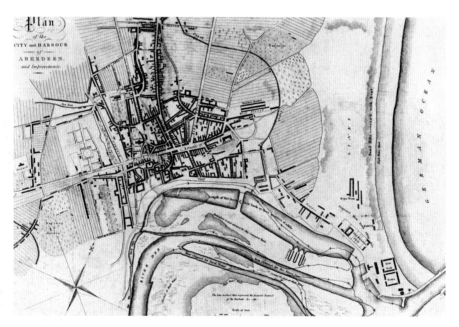

'Plan of the City of Aberdeen and Harbour of Aberdeen and Improvements'. The plan was drawn in 1810 when the North Pier and Round House were well established along with the shipyards at Footdee. The line of the old quay is shown along the south of the city while harbour improvements for the provision of a much larger wet dock is also indicated. Much, but not all of these engineering works, were developed over the next half century.

The expanse of the Dee Estuary is clearly evident in this watercolour painting by J.W. Allen, 1838. The painting is full of the detail of the harbour's life including several rowboats taking passengers and goods to and from Torry and Aberdeen. The old stone harbour works at Point Law are in the centre while the spires of St Nicholas Kirk and the Tolbooth are visible on the skyline.

This view of Aberdeen from Torry during the mid-1870s shows the expansion of the harbour with the River Dee running in its man-made channel. The industrial nature of the port is plain in the number of chimneys and warehouses that stand on or near the quayside. At the centre are the dock gates which maintained high water in the Upper and Victoria Docks.

The clipper *Newcastle* grounded to the south of the harbour mouth on 24 February 1844. Immediately teams of lifeboat men set out under the command of the renowned Arctic whaler, William Penny. Valiant attempts were made by both sets of oarsmen to reach the casualty, only to be rebuffed by the severity of adverse wind and wave. Finally it took the power of the steam paddle tug *Samson* to overcome the force of the storm and rescue all hands. Despite this demonstration of the steam engine's capabilities, Aberdeen's volunteer lifeboat crews persevered with rowed boats until well into the twentieth century.

River Dee ferry boat being wound across the river in this undated lantern slide. Before the building of the Victoria Bridge, the ferry boat was a means of crossing the Dee and the harbour. The Dee ferry is forever associated with the disaster in which thirty-two people drowned when the boat overturned on 5 April 1876.

Andrew Cameron shows off his lifesaving medals and a favoured pet in an 1879 studio photograph. The citation reads, 'Presented to Andrew Cameron for Saving Life in Aberdeen Harbour, 4th October 1879.'

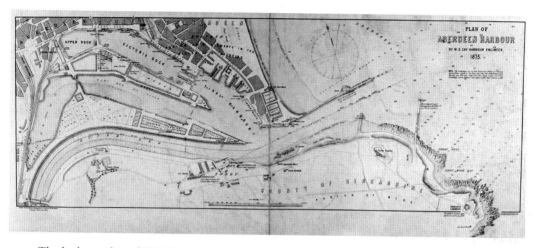

The harbour plan of 1875 by W.D. Cay indicates the full extent of improvements. The Dee is now flowing to the south of its original course, allowing for the creation of the Albert Basin ready for the steam trawler boom that was commencing. Dock gates at Footdee made the Victoria Basin non-tidal, thus solving the problem of large ship mooring. The network of rail and road links completed the scheme to rebuild the port ready for trade, shipbuilding and the fishing industries of the thriving city.

Opposite above: The diverting of the River Dee in the 1870s was the most significant engineering feat of the nineteenth century. It almost doubled the size of the harbour by allowing the creation of the Albert Basin and solved a number of long-term navigation problems. The half mile-long graceful curve of the channel was bridged by the Victoria Bridge while the estuary area to the west of the Albert Basin was filled in, creating valuable land for railway connections to the docks and ancillary maritime industries.

Opposite below: Looking east along the Upper Dock towards the old Regent Bridge *c.*1870. A Banff-registered herring fish boat is joined by both steamships and sailing ships, indicating the breadth of commerce in the port.

The Leading Lights located in Torry are aligned so that they form a line of sight through the centre of the navigation channel at the harbour entrance. The graceful iron towers were built in 1842 and still serve to guide vessels safely into port in an age of precise satellite navigation. The lights show red when the port is open and green when it is closed or unsafe to proceed. View from the west tower of the Leading Lights looking towards the east tower c.1885.

Opposite above: The harbour with the Regent swing bridge in the foreground and HMS *Clyde* in the Victoria Basin, c.1905. *Clyde* was a Royal Navy frigate fitted with a full deckhouse enclosure and used as a training vessel until 1910. The shipyards at Footdee with their tall sheerlegs are visible in the distance.

Opposite below: The naval training ship HMS *Clyde* in the Victoria Dock c.1890. The old warship had a fully enclosed deckhouse that permitted the vessel to be used by cadets for training. The *Clyde* was moored in the harbour between 1890 and 1910, off what is now called Clyde Street. Apart from its primary function, the vessel was used for a variety of social events.

The view from the North Pier during the 1870s provided the opportunity to see the removal of the old south breakwater and the construction of the new one. A large crane stands at the base of the new breakwater (in the distance) and a temporary gantry is in place to facilitate large stones to be delivered to the end of the pier. A bucket dredger works at the site of the old breakwater.

The harbour mouth as seen from the Round House at the base of the North Pier c.1900. The tall brick built structure in the foreground is known colloquially as 'Scarty's Monument', named after one of the harbour pilots of the Victorian era and believed by some to be an aid to navigation. It is in fact an air vent for the sewerage system that ran beneath the site and emptied directly into the harbour channel.

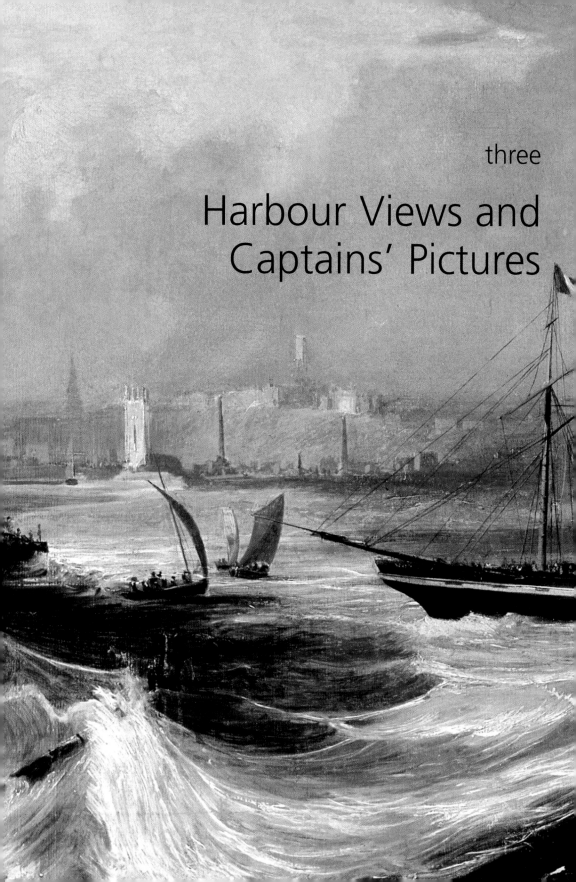

three

Harbour Views and Captains' Pictures

The city north of the expansive Dee Estuary, in the painting 'The View of Aberdeen' by William Mosman, 1756. Allowing for the distinctly odd sense of perspective with figures towering over cottages and ships that are clearly mismatched to the size of the port, the work provides a remarkable insight into the harbour at the time. The River Dee still dominated the operations of the harbour with large areas difficult to navigate at low tide. The main quays were along the north shore where they had first been laid out in medieval times. Over the next fifty years a series of major engineering projects would transform Mosman's Aberdeen into a more complex, efficient and busy port.

'New Aberdeen' portrayed by the famous Scottish painter Alexander Nasmyth c.1817. The 'New' Aberdeen referred to the town built on the River Dee which developed into the thriving port city in the nineteenth century. Old Aberdeen lay to the north and centred on the university and St Machar Cathedral, close to the much smaller river Don.

'The Harbour Mouth' 1838 by J. W. Allen shows an idyllic, almost completely pastoral, scene with a hint of the city and the Dee visible between the arboreal canopy. In reality the harbour was experiencing a period of works that expanded operations and allowed for an increase in commerce and trade. The Hall brothers were experimenting with their revolutionary clipper bow and Thomas Telford had his plans for the lengthening of the North Pier accepted. Allen's view is still valid today with portions of the areas shown along the Dee by the Duthie Park still as verdant as seen here.

Since medieval times, the Shiprow was the principal thoroughfare between Aberdeen's market place at the Castlegate and the harbour. As a sign of the city's mercantile wealth, Robert Watson had the substantial stone house built on Shiprow in 1593. A century later, John Ross of Arnage, a ship merchant and Lord Provost of Aberdeen, lived in the house which now bares his name. This 1880s watercolour by P.L. Forbes depicts the home on the left at a time when it had been divided into tenement homes. Aberdeen's heritage has been showcased in the city's Maritime Museum which incorporates Provost Ross's House.

Above: A Scottish warship *c.*1660. An intriguing painting from the Aberdeen Shipmaster Society collection is believed to be of a Dutch-built vessel in service as a unit of the Scottish Navy. The artist is unknown, as is the original provenance, but recent research suggests that this could have been one of the fleet of ships that sailed for Panama in 1695 as part of the disastrous attempt to establish a Scottish colony at Darien in Panama.

Opposite top: The *Smithfield* was built in 1842, three years after the pioneering 'Aberdeen bow' was used by James and William Hall in their *Scottish Maid*. This oil painting by Arthur Smith shows the tidy brig passing the newly completed Girdleness Lighthouse, just south of the harbour entrance. Hall's design for a swift sailing ship hull was applied to larger craft, which led to the first transoceanic British clipper ship by the late 1840s.

Opposite middle: The brig *Earl of Carlisle* was built in Aberdeen for the Baltic and European trade in 1854. The watercolour shows the vessel off Naples with Mount Vesuvius emitting volcanic smoke and ash in the background.

Opposite bottom: This painting is by the renowned marine artist John Huggins and shows the *Neptune* passing the recently completed Girdleness Lighthouse in 1842. *Neptune* is flying the flag of the Aberdeen White Star Line, the shipping fleet that became world renowned for its fast tea clippers. Huggins typically painted an accurate rendition of a sailing ship being prepared for completion of its voyage. Crewmen are aloft taking in sail, while a side-paddle tug ventures past the North Pier to tow the ship through the narrow harbour entrance.

Earl of Beaconsfield Alestria Naples 1882

This ship portrait shows the wool clipper *British Merchant* bound for Australia, painted by J.C. Ogilvie in 1856. The ship was built by the local yard of John Duthie and served the Duthie Line until only 1860, when she caught fire in Sydney harbour and became a total loss. Ogilvie portrays the clipper encircled by a small fleet of working vessels typical of the period. To the right is a side paddle steamer finishing a voyage from Shetland while fishermen struggle with their nets in the foreground. A Dutch trader and paddle tug appear to the left, with glimpses of the city just visible through the rigging. The artist's signature is inscribed on the flotsam.

Randolph, painted by the Aberdeen artist R.B. Spencer. This ship is listed in Lloyd's Register of Shipping as being built in 1864 for trade to India and New Zealand. As in most of Spencer's works the ship is depicted under full sail in the English Channel off Dover Castle. Although he always signed and dated his paintings, Spencer's use of Dover serves as a secondary confirmation of the painting's authenticity.

Queen of Nations in a typhoon in the South China Seas *c.*1861. Painted by an unknown artist, it shows the clipper ship heeling to starboard in extreme weather. This depiction of a vessel in perilous seas is in marked contrast to the sedate 'captain's pictures' that form the vast majority of ship's portraits. One suspects that this was commissioned by an officer keen to show the mastery of his ship and crew over the worst of nature's storms.

No photograph or painting exists of Aberdeen's most famous ship, *Thermopylae*, in the port of Aberdeen itself. Not unusually for ships built for foreign trade, *Thermopylae*'s first voyage out of Aberdeen was also the last. The watercolour by Eric Berryman was commissioned by Aberdeen Maritime Museum in 1996 to show the great ship on the day of its maiden voyage to London under the command of Captain William Edward. A side-paddle tug waits alongside at the ready to assist the clipper to the North Sea while the companie's Aberdeen White Star house flag is raised aloft.

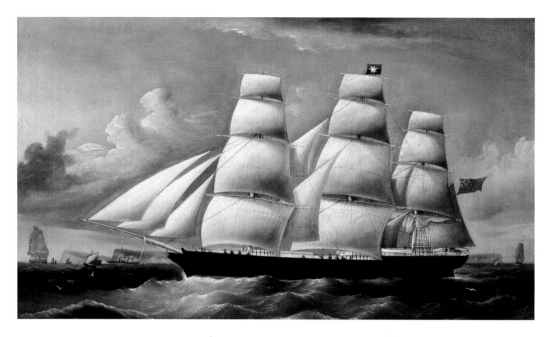

Phoenician was one of the classically named Phoenician was one of the classically named ships of George Thompson Junior's world class Aberdeen White Star Line. Built by Thompson's favoured yard, Walter Hood & Co. in 1847, the Phoenician served in the wool trade and brought back some of the first gold from Australia in 1851. This ship's portrait is by W. Webb and dates from the time of the gold rush.

Many of the vessels built and owned by the Duthie family were designed for the Australian trade. Often a mere 218ft in length, these well run ships with their distinctive Duthie black sided hulls would routinely sail the 12,000 miles in less than four months. Often their destination would be Sydney, and the sight of Sydney Heads were a most welcome indication of a successful voyage. The view of Abergeldie passing the Heads was possibly painted by her master, John Duthie, in 1870.

The paddle steamship *Duke of Richmond* heading north from Aberdeen, painted by Arthur Smith, 1843. Sailings from Aberdeen to Wick, Orkney and Shetland were frequent and reliable thanks to the introduction of steam power to the fleet in the 1830s. Both passengers and business benefited from the service which also connected with ports to the south. The *Duke of Richmond* was eventually wrecked near the mouth of the river Don, close to the area visible behind the ship in this painting, on 8 October 1859.

This painting is very much a propaganda piece. While sailing vessels are being tossed to and fro on the turbulent sea, the steamer *Sovereign* majestically rides the waves on an even keel to the safety of the harbour. At a time when steam power was still new technology in north-east Scotland, the travelling public needed reassurance of the safety, comfort and reliability of *Sovereign* and her companion vessels which made the regular run north and south of Aberdeen.

Above: The spectacular loss of the paddle steamer *Brilliant* on the North Pier brought the townsfolk of Aberdeen to that stormy scene in their hundreds on 12 December 1839. The viewers of the calamity of exploding boilers and falling funnel are also witnesses to a bizarre episode of rivalry in free enterprise. Some of the cargo is orderly being transferred to carts on the pier while more crates are finding their way into the water where two boat crews are eagerly scooping up the flotsam. The following week, adverts appeared in the *Aberdeen Journal* from rival entrepreneurs, announcing the sale of genuine wreck goods from the *Brilliant* and denouncing each other as dealing in inferior material. The ship itself, one of the early 'North Boats' to Shetland and Orkney, was a total loss with her master being the sole fatality.

Above: The Wreck of the Prince Consort was captured in a small oil sketch by the renowned Aberdeen painter Sir George Reid, just after the event on 11 March 1863. The paddle steamer was a veteran of the Northern Isles service and its master and crew knew the hazards of the route, in particular the narrow and tricky entrance to Aberdeen. On this occasion a south-east wind and ebb tide forced the steamer against the North Pier, causing the vessel to founder.

Below: The entrance to Aberdeen harbour, seen from the Torry side, was painted by William Cassie during the 1870s. To the right, a crane is working on the South Breakwater, while gulls circle over fishing nets drying at Footdee to the left. The stone built Round House, one of Aberdeen harbour's most distinctive buildings, was used by the harbour pilots and for control of vessels venturing through the narrow channel. A ubiquitous side-paddle tug is towing a brig into port while the sails of 'Fifie' and 'Zulu' class herring boats are just visible on the horizon.

Opposite below: The wreck of the whaling ship *Oscar* at Greyhope Bay off Girdleness in 1813 with the loss of forty-two souls was deeply felt by the townsfolk of Aberdeen. The destruction of the ship with all but two of her crew so close to home added to the despondency felt by the fishing community.

A tiny watercolour sketch of the launch of the *Port Jackson* from the Alexander Hall shipyard captures the immediacy of the event on 1 August 1882. The impression of excited crowds craning to view the large iron hull enter the water for the first time is made with economy and skill by John Mitchell.

The *Port Jackson* was Aberdeen's only four-masted barque. It was one of the largest sailing vessels and also one of the last to be built in the city. By the 1880s shipyards order books were filled with steam trawlers calling an end to Aberdeen's great age of sail. This ship's portrait by an unknown artist is unusual in that it is a watercolour rather than an oil painting.

One of the most popular paintings of Aberdeen is David Farquharson's 1888 view of the harbour 'The Herring Fleet Leaving the Dee'. The herring fleet was made up of large wooden lug sail rigged 'Fifies' and 'Zulus' which followed the annual herring migration down the North Sea coast. To the left are the River Dee and Victoria Bridge. Fish processing smokehouses are visible at Point Law in the centre of the painting. Aberdeen's shipyards and Round House at the North Pier are on the right.

The *New Victoria Bridge*, painted by James Watt in 1884, was opened on 2 July 1881 to provide a wide carriageway between Aberdeen and Torry over the new course of the River Dee. The 1880s witnessed the diversion of the river into the man-made river channel seen in the painting, as well as a massive boom in population and commerce through the mechanisation of steam trawling. As people flocked to the city in their thousands to work as fishers or processors, tenements sprang up in Torry to accommodate this expansion. A new bridge was necessary to provide a permanent and safe link between Torry and Aberdeen.

Herring Harvest, oil by Archibald Reid, *c.*1873. Once the herring had been caught they were brought ashore where teams of 'herring lassies' worked with incredible speed cleaning, gutting and packing the fish into barrels. Coopers assisted by filling the barrels with brine and fitting the barrel top securely into position ready for export to North European ports. This painting depicts the herring harvest at Gardenstown on the Moray Firth.

Colour postcard of the harbour c.1870. This shows how much the Victorian engineers had rebuilt the quays over a relatively short space of time. The harbour is now ready for the new steamers that would be set to dominate shipping and transform traffic and trade in the coming years.

Kilrenny was probably painted by Alexander Harwood around the time she was built in 1897. Harwood worked as a fish porter for fifty years and was obsessed with the boats that provided his livelihood. He undoubtedly knew every trawler and line boat that used the fish market and would deal with their crews daily. Harwood's passion was in painting detailed and accurate depictions of these vessels, sometimes as commissions and often on spec', and selling them to crew members.

An unknown but accomplished marine artist was commissioned by the Duthie family to execute this ship's portrait of the 1860 *Rifleman*. An exquisite vessel, well designed for great distance travel, the 200ft-long ship gained dubious notoriety in 1873 when her master, Captain Longmuir, was murdered by the steward off the coast of Brazil en route to Australia. The first officer, George Morgan, earned the respect of his peers by bringing the ship to Sydney under such unusual and difficult circumstances. Morgan was given a gold watch by the owners, Longmuir's family received £700 from public subscription while the steward Wilhelm Krauss was found guilty and hung in a Sydney gaol.

The iron paddle steamer *Duke of Sutherland* was wrecked within 20 yards of the North Pier on 1 April 1853. While thousands of townsfolk witnessed the unfolding events, thirty-six passengers were rescued by the lifeboat service and lifelines, leaving sixteen to die as the ship was battered by a south-easterly gale. Such was the sense of outrage that a public petition was organised, and a public enquiry resulted in a vastly improved life saving service.

The *Xenia* was a Danish steamship that went aground off the small fishing village of Collieston, fifteen miles north of Aberdeen on 1 February 1903. Alexander Harwood's dramatic watercolour shows the fishermen of Whinneyfolds rowing out to rescue all hands from the foundering vessel. Such was the gratitude of the Danes that each of the lifesavers was awarded a medal from the King of Denmark.

The entire crew of the Danish steamship *Xenia* pictured after their rescue. The inscription reads 'The crew of the SS *Xenia* rescued through the gallantry and courage of the Whinneyfolds fishermen and the hospitality of their wives and daughters send this as a small token of their gratitude and esteem'.

Barbara Robb by Alexander Harwood, 1930.

The House Flag of the trawler *Terrier*, taken from the original design book of the Hall Russell & Co. shipyard, 1905. Like most yards, Hall Russell would construct the entire vessel for the owner and fit the ship out with all that was needed to go to sea, right down to the teapots, pans and flags.

'*Ben Screel* Sea Trials off Aberdeen' watercolour by George Wiseman, 1957. The *Ben Screel* was one of many 'Ben Boats' built for deep-sea waters. She was owned by Richard Irvin until finally scrapped in 1976.

The *Ben Gairn* painted by George Wiseman, 1961. Wiseman specialised in watercolours and was often commissioned to paint trawlers built by John Lewis & Sons. Sometimes he was able to finish his painting before the vessel was completed by using the ship's plans and his knowledge of these deepwater trawlers. The *Ben Gairn* was one of Richard Irvin & Sons Ltd 'Ben Boats'.

Ben Heilem A 553 portrayed in a watercolour by George Wiseman, 1961. The Lewis-built trawler was 135ft long and like most of the 'Ben Boats', her registration numbers added up to thirteen.

Howard Johnson, the former director of Hall Russell & Co., painted ships under construction in the yard in the early 1950s as in this oil painting. The work captures the shipyard during the post-war boom in ship construction, with two large motor ships nearing completion on the slips. Hall Russell were building some of their largest ships at this time with vessels like the 370ft-long *Sugar Producer* and *Sugar Carrier*.

The trawler *Summerlee* heading to sea past the North Pier in the early 1970s. The vessel was built by the John Lewis shipyard in 1956 and was later owned by Craig Stores Ltd and British United Trawlers. The trawler was scrapped in 1978.

The rebuilding of the historic Round House forms the backdrop to this 1960s view of the trawler *Westerdale*. The roof of the octagonal Round House was extended upward to provide space for the main navigation control centre which overlooks the harbour entrance and into the main basin and docks.

The *Clova* was built for the Clova Fishing Co. Ltd by John Lewis of Aberdeen in 1960. The trawler was later converted to an offshore standby safety vessel which often happened in the oil industry's early years. This 1970s picture also shows cranes loading a large freighter, with North Boats *St Clement* and *St Magnus* in the background.

Aberdeen Harbour Mudtanks watercolour and pencil by Tony Clayden, 1985. These imposing tall tanks that line several of the oil service area quays hold drilling 'mud'. The 'mud' is actually an expensive mixture which is pumped down drill holes to lubricate and cool the drill bit. Oil supply vessels pump the mud onboard from these tanks ready for transfer to rigs and platforms offshore.

Above: The modern oil harbour of 'Europe's Energy Capital' is clearly evident in this 1997 watercolour by Tony Clayden. Oil supply and anchor handling vessels are, size-for-size, some of the most powerful ships afloat. Their vast bulk and bright high visibility paint schemes cannot fail to impress. The vessels pictured are *Huntetor, Havila Chieftain, Havila Castle* and the P&O ferry, *St Clair.*

Below: The hard-hatted shipyard workers silhouetted in the light of the building shed witness to the launch of ship number 1,000 at Hall Russell. The days of Aberdeen's long shipbuilding history ended on 31 October 1989 with the launch of RMS *St Helena* from the covered slipway of the former Hall Russell & Co. By this time the yard had been taken over by A&P Appledore and efforts to secure orders were meeting without success. Sadly for the workforce the *St Helena* launched that day by the Duke of York was to be the last ship built in Aberdeen, completing a 200-year history of almost 3,000 ship launches.

Above: The *Statesman* is berthed at Regent Quay next to the Aberdeen Harbour offices, with its distinctive clock tower, 2001. Such vessels have become a familiar sight in the port for three decades and they provide a major economic boost to the city and region. The ships are built to deliver a multiplicity of tasks from supplying materials to offshore installations to towing rigs to different oil and gas fields in the North Sea. Other specialised vessels give support to divers and remotely operated vehicles.

Left: The *Murchison* oil production platform model stands through three floors of the Aberdeen Maritime Museum. The topsides section above the waterline dates from 1979 when it was constructed as an engineering model to ensure the miles of pipes would not clash. Teams of model makers worked with designers on this model in the era before computers could cope with three-dimensional engineering problems. The museum refurbished the topsides and added the jacket section, below the waterline, to recreate the oil platform as it was when inaugurated in 1980. The *Murchison* model is the world's largest oil industry model, rising 8.5m through the museum floors.

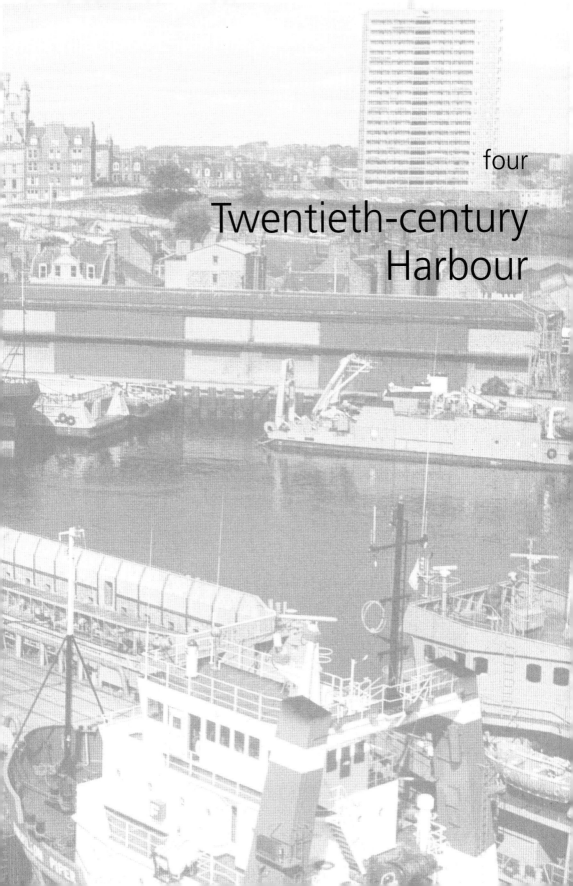

four

Twentieth-century
Harbour

The bucket dredger *Annie W. Lewis* off Pocra Quay with the Round House and navigation channel in the background. *Annie W. Lewis* was a familiar sight in the harbour from 1927 to the late 1960s. The constant clatter of the buckets as they scooped sand and mud from the harbour was a familiar sound throughout the city for half a century. The locally built dredger would dump her cargo far enough off the coast to ensure that the silt would not be swept back toward the harbour.

Grab Dredger No. 2 was used in the harbour to keep enough depth at the quaysides for ships as they loaded cargo. This dredger, pictured dumping silt, sand and mud off Aberdeen, was built by Alexander Hall & Co. in 1931.

The side-paddle tug *Fairweather* on a trial trip in Aberdeen Bay *c*.1910. *Fairweather* was a stalwart of harbour operations, providing towing services for all manner of vessels in need of assistance.

Pile driving new quays along Market Street in the 1930s. Aberdeen Harbour Board has been responsible for the development and improvement of the port since medieval times and the rebuilding of quays has been a constant engineering task for centuries. Changes such as these resulted in deepwater quays being available throughout most of the harbour by the late twentieth century.

A collier unloading on the south side of the Upper Dock *c*.1930. Coal lorries and horse-drawn carts await their loads of bags of domestic coal for the city's population. The back of the Regent Bridge engine house is on the right, while the Salvation Army Citadel is just visible below the ship's grab bucket.

View along Market Street and the Upper Dock at 10.15 a.m., 10 June 1939. The close proximity of the harbour and city is clearly apparent as cars and cycles mingle with lorries and horse-drawn carts unloading timber.

A great storm in the winter of 1936 breached the south breakwater that had protected the harbour entrance for sixty years. The breakwater is essential for keeping the entrance navigable and therefore a rebuilding of the structures was necessary before the next winter's gales and a 'Titan' crane was constructed on site to facilitate repairs.

A rare view of the Grand Fleet off Aberdeen's south breakwater *c.*1914. Despite its strategic position, Aberdeen's harbour was far too small to accommodate the Royal Navy's largest ships and the bay provided no defence against attack. The Fleet is seen en route either to or from the main anchorage at Scapa Flow.

Opposite above: The massive 'Titan' crane receives its official test ready for the reconstruction of the South Breakwater, 5 July 1937.

Opposite below: The crane deftly moves a huge masonry block into position.

A member of the Duthie family enjoys the sun on Aberdeen beach at very low tide *c.*1900. The picture shows the extreme lengths people would take to avoid exposing any part of their person apart from the face. The large bathing house is in the background.

A crowded pleasure beach is shown in this picture postcard entitled 'The Call of the Seaside', from the 1920s. The large bathhouse is to the left with the beach ballroom on the right.

The natural long curving beach just a mile from the city centre was an attraction to Aberdonians and visitors alike for a long time. This 1930s leaflet advertises 'the Silver City with the Golden Sands'.

Aerial view of the Upper Dock and fish market, Albert Basin c.1930. The dock gates and Regent Bridge are clearly visible as well as city centre landmarks such as the Town House, Aberdeen Harbour Board offices and the central railway station on Guild Street.

Aerial view of Torry dock and harbour *c.*1930. The Victoria Bridge spans the long curve of the River Dee channel. The tenements of Torry stand out in lines built up from the line of the river. The white towers of the Leading Lights (left) are well defined in the summer sunshine.

Aerial view of the Footdee shipyards (right) and St Clement's church (left) *c*.1930. Beyond the industrialised area by the quayside lies the unspoiled natural line of the beach and an amusement park.

Aerial view of the harbour from the south-west, *c*.1930. At this vantage point above the Dee and Torry, the steam trawlers either side of Point Law, the floating Pontoon Dock at Footdee and a dozen slipways at the Alexander Hall and Hall Russell shipyards in the distance are all visible.

The oil boom brought a fleet of oil services ships to the port which can be seen at the upper harbour, 1978. Both supply and diving support vessels are berthed during the dramatic period of growth in the sector. As was the case 100 years earlier with the trawler boom, the city coped successfully with the demands on local industries, housing and infrastructure the flourishing offshore industry made on Aberdeen.

Loading rig anchor chain aboard the offshore supply vessel *Far Senior* at the Telford Dock, 8 October 1999. The large load capacity of these powerful ships is apparent as well as the operational bridge overlooking the deck. Controls are duplicated at this side of the double-ended bridge to allow the ship to carry out precise manoeuvres close to offshore installations.

five

Coastal Craft

The first *St Sunniva* aground at Torry was successfully re-floated, but then had the misfortune to be wrecked on Mousa, Shetland on 10 April 1930. Although the ship was a total loss, all onboard were rescued and the vessel itself was replaced within the year by *St Sunniva* II, a graceful vessel that was a close replica of her forbearer. The wreck only serves to emphasise how treacherous the waters the North Boats encountered on a regular basis were and, despite modern navigation equipment and experienced crews, accidents did occur.

Opposite above: Launch of the *St Sunniva* II from Hall Russell & Co., 2 April 1931. The order of this 'North Boat' was placed following the loss of *St Sunniva* I on 10 April the previous year. The completion of the replacement vessel in such quick time during the Great Depression is very impressive. The yacht-like appearance made the *St Sunniva* a popular ship for both cruises, and on her regular voyages between ports in the North of Scotland.

Opposite below: Crew of the 'North Boat' *St Nicholas* in late 1890. The only man identified is stoker William Paterson (back row, second left). A curious boy peeks at the camera from the hold, unbeknown to the crew. *St Nicholas* operated between Aberdeen and the Northern Isles between 1871 and 1914 when she ran aground at Wick, becoming a total loss.

The *St Sunniva* II in her summer livery, *c.*1932. This graceful steamer served on the route to Shetland for most of the year while her predecessor ventured as far as St Petersburg and the Mediterranean. *St Sunniva* II was requisitioned as a convoy rescue vessel during the Second World War and was lost with all hands in the icy waters off Newfoundland on 21-22 January 1943.

Figurehead of *St Sunniva* II, Aberdeen, in the 1930s. *St Sunniva* had a detachable arm that could be removed in heavy weather. The Hall Russell built steamship was one of the most beautiful of Aberdeen's ships with clipper bow, raked funnel and masts lending a yacht-like appearance to the vessel. The sheerlegs at Waterloo Quay are busy with the fit-out of recently launched steamers.

St Sunniva II heads to sea past the South Breakwater in the 1930s. The yacht-like steamer served on the regular run to Shetland until requisitioned by the Admiralty during the Second World War.

The North of Scotland & Orkney & Shetland Steam Navigation Co. had a long tradition of using their vessels for summer cruises around the Scottish coast and across the North Sea. The cruises were conveniently linked with the rail network, thereby opening the market to tourists throughout Britain. This advertisement came from the 1939 Centenary booklet.

S. S. "Hogarth."   Torpedoed in the North Sea on 8th June, 1918.

The Aberdeen Steam Navigation Company's fine Passenger Steamers sailing between London and Aberdeen every Wednesday and Saturday.

The Aberdeen Steam Navigation Co. operated their 'London Boats' service on a regular basis using steamships like the *Aberdonian* and *Hogarth*, pictured here. This picture postcard has been overprinted to note that the *Hogarth* was sunk in enemy action on 8 June 1918. The official war record puts the sinking a day earlier, ten miles off Langstane while Aberdeen bound.

St Clair II making her way over the 'bar' at the harbour entrance during a 'Nor' easter' on Wednesday 11 November 1950. *St Clair* was a stalwart of the North Boat service from 1937 to 1967, also seeing war service as HMS *Baldur*. Photograph courtesy of *Aberdeen Journals*

THE
ABERDEEN STEAM NAVIGATION
COMPANY LIMITED

The finely-equipped passenger carrying vessels of this Company.
" LOCHNAGAR " and "ABERDONIAN,"
give a service of two sailings each week (from Aberdeen and London, every Wednesday and Saturday), June to September inclusive, affording the cheapest, healthiest, and most enjoyable means of travel.

The accommodation for both First and Second Cabin Passengers is very superior. The ordinary passage lasts about 36 hours. Passengers who wish to do so may sleep on board in London at the following extra cost- **Bed and Break-fast—1st Cabin, 7/6; 2nd Cabin, 5/-**

PASSAGE FARES

FIRST CABIN		SECOND CABIN	
Single Tickets - £2 10 0		Single Tickets - £1 7 6	
Do. (Children under 14 years) £1 5 0		Do. (Children under 14 years) £0 18 4	
Return Tickets		Return Tickets	
(available for Three Months) £3 15 0		(available for Three Months) £2 0 0	
Do. (Children under 14 years) £1 17 6		Do. (Children under 14 years) £1 6 8	

PRIVATE CABINS, four-berthed, let on the following special terms, subject to accommodation being available:—

If occupied by—

Three Passengers, Single Fare £8 5 0 Return Fare £12 0 0
Two Passengers, Single Fare £6 0 0 Return Fare £ 8 10 0
One Passenger, Single Fare £5 0 0 Return Fare £ 7 10 0

In addition to the usual accommodation, a limited number of Two-berthed Deck Cabins and Cabins-de-Luxe on the " LOCHNAGAR " can be booked at slightly increased Fares. There are Dining Saloons for Second Cabin Passengers on both vessels.

The Company's Tender, " ICH DIEN," carries passengers free of charge between Westminster Pier and the Company's Wharf at Limehouse—a most instructive and enjoyable run.

Meals are of excellent quality, and every passenger may rely on receiving perfect attention and courtesy,

Full particulars of Sailings with Lists of Fares will be furnished and passages booked on application to

EDWARD J. SAVAGE, Manager
87 Waterloo Quay, Aberdeen

Telephone No. 7

12

Advertisement for the Aberdeen Steam Navigation Co., 1935.

Opposite above: The Aberdeen, Newcastle & Hull Steam Co. passenger and cargo ship SS *Highlander* from a picture postcard of the 1920s. The 243ft-long *Highlander* was built by Caledon of Dundee in 1916.

Opposite below: SS *Aberdonian* was one of a small fleet of ships owned by the Aberdeen Steam Navigation Co.. Popularly known as the 'London Boats', the like of *Aberdonian* provided regular services between Aberdeen, Newcastle and London. Not all her passengers were human; ample accommodation was designed for prime Aberdeen Angus cattle for their trip to the London markets. Fares for passengers varied according to how close the accommodation was to the cattle hold!

S.S. HIGHLANDER.

This luxurious Passenger Steamer sails Aberdeen to Newcastle & Hull every Saturday
returning from Hull every Wednesday and from Newcastle every Thursday.

~ Aberdeen Newcastle & Hull Steam Co. Ld. Aberdeen. ~

S.S. "ABERDONIAN."

The Aberdeen Steam Navigation Company's fine Passenger
Steamers sailing between London & Aberdeen every
Wednesday & Saturday.

Copyright.
Robertson, Photo, Aberdeen.

six

Shipbuilding

One of maritime history's outstanding photographs shows a cross-section of Alexander Hall shipyard staff in front of two new builds, the *Coulmakyle* and *Natal Star*, in 1862. The owner's family members, James and Alexander, are standing to the right behind two office boys. Draughtsmen and shipwrights are to the left while two seated men at the centre hold a bible between them, symbolic of a contract between staff. The photograph is unusual in that it brings together the range of experiences within a nineteenth-century shipyard while showing the conditions in which the vessels themselves were built.

Alexander Hall staff pose informally in front of some of the yard outbuildings on the same day as the previous photograph. With wood the principal building material, fire was a constant and real threat. Rows of water buckets stand in readiness while the star shaped insurance badge to the left shows that the yard is protected by the fire brigade. Five years later fire did break out, threatening the firm's largest ever order, *Jho-Sho-Maru*. The ship was moved and the fire extinguished but the exertions caused the owner, James Hall, to collapse and die of heart failure.

A very early photograph of the Alexander Hall Footdee shipyard from the mid-nineteenth century. The end of a slipway is visible on the beach front, showing the rudimentary way in which vessels of the era were constructed. Most striking are the whale arches situated in the gardens. Formed from the jaws of Greenland 'Right Whales', these arches featured in several Aberdeen locations, even into the 1980s. At the time of the photograph Aberdeen was still a major whaling port although Dundee and Peterhead were to overtake the city in the later half of the nineteenth century.

A primary tool of the shipbuilding industry was the half model. Here, Robert Duthie is carefully shaping the graceful hull form that would soon be scaled up to build the full ship during the 1860s. Half models were a means of referencing not only the shape of the hull but positions of frames and latterly the plates of iron ships. They were so precise that the shipwrights working in the mould loft could scale-up directly from the model to the full size vessels.

The moulding loft at Duthie's shipyard in the 1920s. Once the ship had been designed, shipwrights would scale up the ship's frames on the moulding floor using thin pieces of wood and tracing the lines on the floor of the loft. The wooden templates would then go to the steel fabricators for making up into the full size elements of the ship. Concentration, experience and skill were prerequisites for working in the loft.

Above: The SS *Aberdeen* in the graving dock *c.*1890. The dock was constructed in 1885 to give the port a large repair facility. It could often take several smaller ships at one time or a ship the size of the 230ft-long *Aberdeen*. The dock was located at Point Law and served the harbour until its function was taken over by a floating pontoon dock and repair slips at Footdee.

Opposite above: Hall Russell & Co. drawing office *c.*1929. The team of draughtsmen worked on the production of hundreds of technical drawings necessary in the design of any ship. Each drawing had to be precise and to scale in order for the machine shop operatives, moulders and shipwrights to manufacture the tens of thousands of parts that went to build the ship. There was no room for error, hence the importance of the drawing office staff to the shipyard

Opposite below: John Lewis & Sons shipyard workers in the engine shed, *c.*1920.

Above: The graving dock provided large ship repair facilities for thirty years. By 1915 it was felt to be redundant due to the introduction of the floating pontoon dock which provided a flexible means of facilitating ship repairs. There were also two dry docks at the Footdee shipyards so by the time of this photograph, 30 July 1925, demolition work on the old graving dock was well underway.

Opposite above: The maiden voyage of the SS *Thermopylae* in 1892 was advertised by the sale of raffle tickets for an oil painting of the new vessel. This ticket is promoted by an office on Shiprow, close to the site of the Aberdeen Maritime Museum. The steamer that carried the name of Aberdeen's greatest tea clipper was destined to take passengers and cargo to Australia. She was eventually wrecked off Cape Town, South Africa, on 11 September 1899.

Opposite below: Pontoon dock No.3 berthed at Pocra Quay on 8 June 1956. The floating dock was itself receiving repairs and new steel plates are visible here. Tanks in the pontoon dock were flooded to partially submerge the dock which allowed ships to be positioned over the repair deck. By then pumping out the water the dock and the ship would be lifted and the maintenance work on the vessel started.

No. ....

Name, ...

Address, ...

Date, ...

J. DANIEL & SON, PRINTERS, ABERDEEN.

No. ....

PRIZE DRAWING

OF

Oil Painting of S. S. Thermopylæ off Aberdeen.

DRAWING TO TAKE PLACE

IN THE CAFE, SHIPROW,

On Saturday, 30th December, 1892.

AT FOUR O'CLOCK P.M.

Winning Number to be Advertised in the "**Evening Express**" of Monday, 2nd January, 1893.

TICKETS, 3d. each.

The mass production of steel steam trawlers is evident in this view of the Alexander Hall & Co. shipyard in 1900. The hulls are doubled up on the slipways to conserve space. Production of trawlers, line boats and drifters between 1885 and 1914 amounted to well over half the tonnage built in the city.

The steamship *Idaho* grounded off Aberdeen beach on 9 January 1929. She entered local folklore through her grounding off the Beach Ballroom. The ship was there long enough for the trams to change their destination signs from 'the beach' to 'Idaho'.

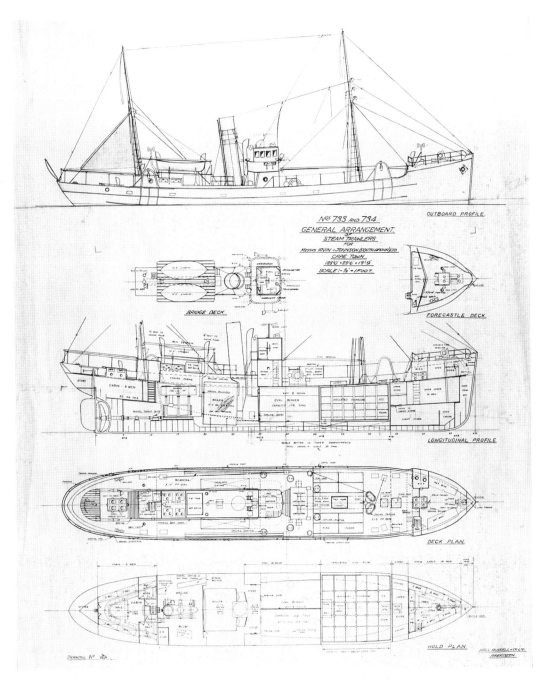

Plan of the trawlers *Aristea* and *Crassula* built as ship numbers 733 and 734 by Hall Russell & Co. in 1935. The General Arrangement drawing served as the main reference drawing for the dozens of detailed plans used by the shipwrights and engineers during the ship's construction. Proving the international reputation of Aberdeen shipbuilders, these vessels were ordered by Irvin and Johnson for South Africa.

A large boiler being prepared for installation into a steamship, possibly the *Intaba*, by use of the sheerlegs at Waterloo Quay *c.*1910. Boilers and engines were only fitted in the ship following launch. The sheerlegs were the only crane arrangement available capable of handling the weight of such heavy pieces of machinery. Only the tripod strength and height of the sheerlegs could have the ability to take such weights from the quay and place them safely onboard the hulls waiting alongside.

Shipyard workers and barmen outside the Neptune Bar on York Place *c.*1900. The bar was a popular pub with the workforce as it was sited in the midst of the major shipyards. Tragedy is associated with the Neptune as several workmen were killed while sheltering in the doorway during a large air raid on the shipyards on 12 July 1940.

The Alexander Hall & Co. football club of 1917/18. The club was one of several teams fielded by Aberdeen's maritime industries. In the case of the Hall FC, success is evident in the form of the trophy.

A riveting team at work by the stern post at the John Lewis & Sons yard, *c.*1940. The 'holder-on' is facing the camera, keeping the hot rivet in position while two men hammer the rivet home. They would work as a team to complete the task quickly in order to produce a waterproof joint between the steel plates and frames.

Opposite: The riveting squad at Hall Russell shipbuilders on board the collier *Spray c.*1932. The riveting team included the 'heater boys' in the foreground, whose job it was to heat the rivets to the correct temperature in an open furnace. They would then pitch the glowing rivet to the 'holder-on' who would position the rivet in the hole and then hold it in position by leaning against it with a special tool. A team of two men would then rhythmically hammer the rivet home. Those in the photograph are, from left to right, back row: Chowter Gowan, Fred Giddings, and Mr Brennan; front row: John McLeod, John Thompson.

Above: One of eight Flower-class corvettes constructed in Aberdeen was the Hall-built HMS *Lavender*, completed in 1941. Designed along the lines of a rugged whale catcher and built in yards in Britain and Canada, the corvettes filled a gap in convoy defence, helping to ensure a constant flow of material and fighting forces to the UK.

Left: A woman grasps a red-hot rivet with a pair of tongs at the John Lewis & Sons shipyard *c.*1940. Women worked in the yards as part of the effort to maintain shipbuilding during the Second World War, performing many of the tasks that had been previously part of an all-male dominated industry.

Sir William Hardy being launched from the Hall Russell & Co. slipway in 1955. The vessel served as a fisheries research vessel for the Ministry of Agriculture & Fisheries. She gained notoriety in 1978 when she was sold to Greenpeace and renamed *Rainbow Warrior*. French Secret Service agents in Auckland harbour blew her up during the campaign to disrupt nuclear weapons testing in the Pacific on 10 July 1985.

STERN TRAWLERS...
...TO OWNERS' REQUIREMENTS

OUR HIGHLY SKILLED TECHNICAL SERVICES ARE AT THE DISPOSAL OF ALL TRAWLER OWNERS WHO MAY BE CONSIDERING MODERNISING THEIR FLEET.

WE HAVE SEVERAL INTERESTING FULLY DEVELOPED DESIGNS FOR THE VARYING NEEDS OF THE FISHING INDUSTRY, INCLUDING BOTH SMALL AND LARGE SEMI-FACTORY SHIPS, FULL FREEZERS AND PART FREEZERS.

Below we illustrate the first and largest Diesel-electric all Refrigerated Stern-Trawler in the United Kingdom, building to the order of J. MARR & SON LTD., HULL

HALL, RUSSELL & CO. LTD.
ALEXANDER HALL & CO. LTD.
ABERDEEN
P.O. BOX 36 • Telephone:– ABERDEEN 29244

Advertisement from *Fishing News International* for Hall Russell and Alexander Hall-built steam trawlers from 1962.

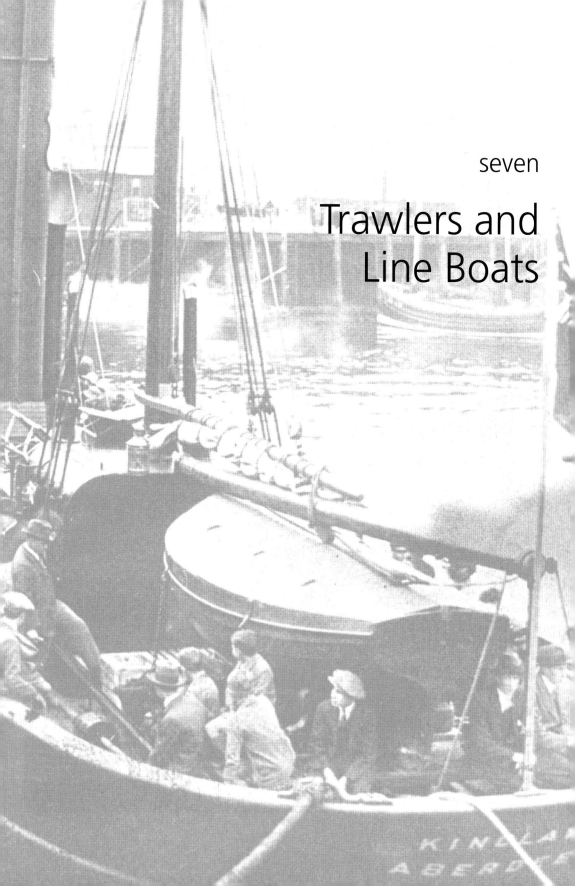

seven

Trawlers and
Line Boats

Christina Lovie Burnett with her creel on her back around 1910. She was one of many fishwives who worked in the fishing industry. Tasks would include collecting and shelling mussels to bait the small line hooks, gutting fish and bringing the catch to market using the creel strapped to her back.

The herring boom of the 1870s through to the First World War brought transient hectic activity to Aberdeen's quayside. As the herring made their annual southerly migration to warmer waters, so too did the fishing fleet of 'Zulus' and 'Fifies' together with the teams of 'herring lassies' who cleaned and packed the catch. Despite the backbreaking work with their hands in cold brine and fish offal, the women's nimble fingers could gut massive amounts of fish. The herring barrels were then filled with brine to preserve the fish for export.

Choir members of St Nicholas church, Aberdeen, dressed as fishwives for singing 'Caller Herrin''. The woman in the centre is wearing a creel that would be used to carry fish to market.

A herring crew dressed up in their best clothes for a studio photograph, 1900. The herring lassies were often shown on postcards in working garb. The cards would be available to send from any of the ports and herring stations visited during the migration. The women here are identified by their fishing 'by-name', from left to right: Lil's Nancy, Lil's Margaret and Mary Meek.

A group of fishermen tippin' sma' lin' (tipping small lines) at Torry harbour *c*.1930. After the small lines of the inshore fisheries had been brought ashore with the catch, the lines had to be disentangled ready to prepare them for baiting. The lines were placed over a 'spull tree' (pole), making it easier to unpick the tangled lines and hooks. Aberdeen's navigation channel and Round House are visible in the distance. (George Leiper)

Mary Christie and her great niece Annie McPherson baiting small lines, back of 90 Abbey Road, Torry. Fishing communities like Footdee and Torry were well within the city but had the atmosphere of smaller fishing villages. Traditional inshore fishing methods ensured family involvement in most aspects of preparation for shooting the small lines. Children would help with the gathering of mussels and the baiting of the lines. (Jim Wood)

Crewmen reddin' (making ready) lines on a great liner during the 1930s. The line boats used lines with hundreds of hooks as the means of catching fish. Before shooting the lines, each hook, line, snood (the line between the great or long line and hook) had to be made ready by disentangling the lines, making repairs and neatly coiling them. The 'reddin'' making ready process was very time consuming as any mistake could cause lines to foul with reduced prospect for a successful catch. (George Leiper)

The trip to Aberdeen Bay to adjust the compass was more an excuse for an outing of family and friends of the crew of the *North King* in the 1920s. While most are obviously enjoying the trip, one man stands atop the wheelhouse seeing to the serious task at hand. Such trial trips were normally the only chance family members had of sharing the experience of a trawler at sea and were treated as festive occasions with plenty of food and drink available. (Jim Wood)

The great liner *Kinclaven* leaving the slipway in 1924. The Duthie shipyard was located in Torry, south of the River Dee with Sinclair Road lying between the yard and the water. On launch day the road was closed while a bridging slip was positioned between the permanent sections on either side. Local people witnessed the unusual spectacle of a ship crossing the road every time the Duthies launched one of their vessels.

A trial trip for a new fishing vessel was cause for great celebration. This was the case of the 1924 line boat *Kinclaven*, shown here with her decks full of crew and their families preparing for a festive trip down the harbour and into Aberdeen Bay. This was the only occasion wives and children had to visit their husband's ship and join the festivities accompanied by a generous supply of food and drink.

The great liner, *Mount Keen*, passing Torry Battery around 1946, after a first trip under the command of skipper George Leiper. Second World War gun batteries are still visible here, immediately after the war. They were part of the city's defences against air raids against the harbour, the shipbuilding yards and shipping. (George Leiper)

Curlew, formerly a great line fishing vessel converted to a trawler, leaving the fish dock on 12 December 1956. The *Curlew* was built as the *Granton N. B.* by Hall Russell in 1912. The vessel was withdrawn from service after a remarkable run of service in 1955.

Mugs of tea at the galley door on board a typical Aberdeen trawler during the 1930s.

Hauling a 'but (halibut) on board the great liner *General Botha* during the 1930s. Line boats used long lines with hundreds of baited hooks to lure halibut and cod. Unlike the trawlers that netted all types and sizes of fish, the liners caught large and healthy fish that would attract premium prices at market. During the years of plentiful supplies, halibut such as this one could take two or three men to haul on deck, using gaffs. (George Leiper)

The *Saxon Prince* was a side-paddle tug called into service as an experimental trawler in the 1880s. Like the first *Toiler* experiment these boats proved that huge catches could be made by running trawl nets from a steam powered vessel. Within five years of the experiments, Aberdeen was constructing dozens of purpose-designed trawlers and servicing a massively expanding mechanised fishing industry. The 'trawler boom' era had arrived.

Many people in maritime trades wanted their photograph taken at their place of work, whether in shipyards or on fishing boats. Usually the ship's life-ring was featured, but in the instance of this 1905 photograph of the *Terrier* crew the scene is completed with the presence of four dogs. The master was obviously a dog lover as the house flag sported the profile of a terrier's head (see page 51).

Crew of the *Ben Voirlich* with the life-ring onboard their new trawler in 1900. The ship was built for Richard Irvin & Sons of Aberdeen and was sold in 1914 to Turkey, being renamed *Eregli*.

The steam trawler *River Lossie* passing the Round House *c.*1950. The Paisley-built vessel was originally a Strath-class Admiralty trawler built for First World War service, but completed too late for service. She was used as an armed patrol vessel during the Second World War and returned to fishing in February 1945. The *River Lossie* grounded on Robbie Ramsay's Baa, Shetland, and became a total loss on 27 March 1953.

The Aberdeen great liner *Lord Talbot* iced up off Greenland in the 1930s. Liners would often make extended trips to waters off Greenland and Iceland to be rewarded with good catches of large halibut. The price for such high-value catches was in the extra time and cost of travel but also the treacherous conditions encountered. An iced up superstructure not only meant additional hazardous work for the crew in chopping the ice off, but potential disaster should the vessel become top heavy with ice threatening to capsize the boat.

The Hutchison family on the deck of the *Lord Talbot*, September 1932. The Americans, dubbed the 'Flying Family', were attempting a transantlantic air trip when their aircraft was forced down on the Greenland coast. After five days in increasingly desperate circumstances, the family, including two daughters – Kathryn aged twelve and Janet Lee aged eight – were rescued by the *Lord Talbot*. The crew were fêted on their return but the master, Tom Watson, was sacked for having broken off from fishing to bring the family back. Such was the public outrage at this that he had no difficulty in obtaining employment with another company.

A steam trawler, seemingly about to be swallowed up by the storm as it attempts to enter Aberdeen harbour. The South Breakwater appears to be more of a navigation hazard than a protective barrier against the force of the wind-lashed sea. Conditions like these are relatively rare but when they do occur the harbour is closed to all traffic. (George Leiper)

The wrecked trawler off the North Pier is not identified on the original photograph. However, it is likely to be the *George Stroud* which was wrecked at that position on Christmas Day 1935. Tragically the skipper James Philips, mate A. Walker and chief engineer Tom Barras all died in the rough and icy waters that day.

An unidentified trawler crossing the 'bar' at the mouth of the harbour around 1930. This sums up the standard conditions encountered by all sizes of craft at the harbour mouth, even in calm conditions. The sand bar, created by tide and currents off the coast, has been a hazard to navigate for as long as vessels have been using the Dee Estuary and later harbour.

Icy conditions in the harbour, *c*.1910. The River Dee often deposits ice into the harbour, where it can be a nuisance but rarely a hazard to navigation.

During Aberdeen's boom period in building and operating steam trawlers, drifters and line boats, the city built almost 1,000 such vessels from the 1880s to the 1960s. Over those years these vessels returned regularly to their home port so that on average hundreds would be using the fish market, victuals, coaling and ice facilities in the course of a week. Evidence of this is seen in this photograph of dozens of trawlers tied up near the Pontoon dock. Similar congestion would occur at the market as vessels could only unload their catch over the bow – such was competition for space. (George Leiper)

A mixture of steam trawlers and sail fishing vessels nudge for dock space in the Albert Basin, June 1901. The sail powered 'Fifies' were part of the herring fleet that fished off Aberdeen in the summer. The fleet and attendant workers followed the herring in their annual migration from north to south.

The Aberdeen-registered *Yorick* on its way to sea in 1948. The *Yorick* was built in Beverley in 1909, surviving not only the rigours of the sea but also two world wars. The life and work of Captain John Buchan and his crew was captured on film for a feature magazine article.

The crew of the trawler *Yorick* enjoying their tea in the ship's tiny mess in 1948. Large mugs of steaming tea are secured by huge fiddles dividing the table into compartments, thus guarding both food and drink from too much spillage in the topsy-turvy world of a working fishing boat in the middle of the North Sea. (William Buchan)

Opposite above: The crew of the *Yorick* are on deck during a 1948 fishing trip. Although bundled up against the cold, it is remarkable to note the lack of standardised protective clothing, particularly in view of the harsh conditions frequently encountered on a vessel with such little shelter areas except the wheelhouse and below deck space. (William Buchan)

Opposite below: A large lump of cold seawater awaits this trawlerman seconds after the shutter snapped to produce this image onboard the *Yorick* in 1948. This is one of a series shot during a typical fishing trip on *Yorick*, which was under the command of skipper John Buchan. (William Buchan)

John 'Johndie' Buchan on the radio telephone on board the trawler *Yorick* in 1948.
Radiotelegraphy had proved its value over the previous quarter century with trawlermen able to
communicate their location and information on weather and fishing grounds. It could prove to be
a lifesaver as assistance could be summoned should vessel and crew be in danger. (William Buchan)

eight

Fish Processing

An auctioneer at the fish market *c.*1900. He is taking bids on the catch with successful bidders being recorded in the notebook in his right hand.

Trinity fish market, as it was in the mid-nineteenth century, with fishwives 'having a news' following the day's trading. All the fish landed would be from sailing trawlers, drifters and inshore line fishing craft with the size of the market reflecting this level of industry. Fishing was very much at the heart of local communities round the coast and Aberdeen was no exception to this.

A picture postcard dated 1914 shows line-caught halibut and cod, graded according to size. Such was the massive involvement by Aberdonians in the fishing industries that the fish market was an attraction in its own right. Pictures of its activities and record catches would frequently be used on postcards.

Trawlers docked at the fish market, Albert Dock *c.*1925. All the trawlers are busy unloading their catch with freshly landed fish boxed and ready for auction under the cover of the market roof.

Halibut laid out in decreasing order of size at Aberdeen fish market in the early 1930s. These halibut were caught by steam line boats that used great lines with hundreds of baited hooks to make their catch. The principal high-value fish caught by this method were the halibut.

Inside the fish market's main warehouse, before the First World War. Boxes of iced fish landed that morning were auctioned and then moved by the buyers to their transport waiting on the other side of the wide doors.

Once the fish left the warehouse it would be taken by the processing companies' own transport to be prepared as fresh fillet fish for the home market, or cured for both the domestic and export trade. The horse and cart transport indicates the date was around 1914.

A fish worker filleting a large cod fish, *c.*1950. Fish processors worked in the city's massive fishing industry in their hundreds. They were a key element in a chain of workers that provided fresh and cured fish for the home and export markets. The rudimentary conditions of their employment is more than obvious in this photograph.

Filleting single haddock at Allen & Dey processors *c*.1950. Filleters had to work quickly to prepare the fish for market in cold, damp conditions. Although machines can now do some of these tasks, the skills and dexterity of a trained 'fish surgeon' are still in demand in Aberdeen.

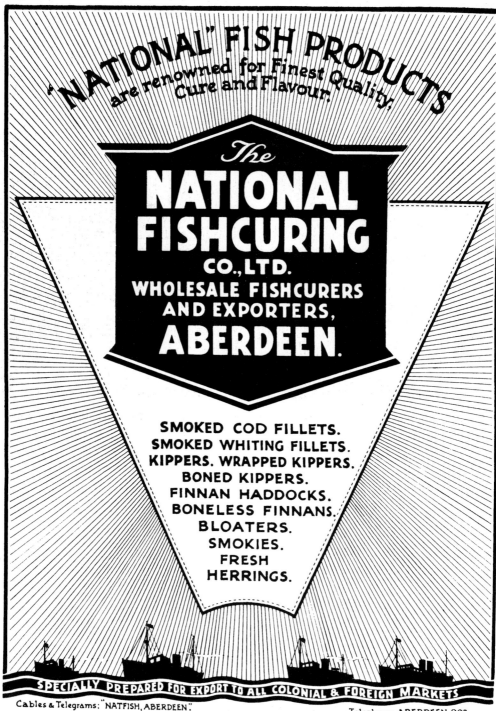

Splitting and cleaning cod fish at the curing works of Williamson & Co. on Sinclair Road. Men and women worked together in preparing the cod for salt curing. A trolley of large split cod is being loaded to the right of the picture.

Opposite: Advertisement for the National Fishcuring Co. Ltd, *c.*1930.

Salt curing of codfish at the No.1 Warehouse, Williamson & Co. The coarse salt is plainly visible on the fish stacked in the foreground while men with prepared split cod are standing on the stacks in the distance.

The premises of Williamson & Co. at the Esplanade next to Victoria Bridge, early 1920s. Williamson was one of the city's principal fish processors and exporters. They specialised in dry cured fish as well as other cures. The horse-drawn and motorised transport in front of the company buildings are loaded with boxes of fresh fish and barrels for wet cured fish.

Company officials of Williamson & Co. inspecting the salt fish store. Here the split fish is still wet. This allows the salt layered between the fish to penetrate.

The extent of the salt cod Williamson & Co. processed largely for export is apparent in the early 1920s publicity shot. The cranes in the background are possibly at the harbour area adjacent to Albert Quay.

The Close Fish Department, Allan & Dey, 1911.

Opposite above: Owners of J. Williamson & Co. examine a split salt cod in the 1930s. It is believed that the owners are showing off their produce to sales representatives in front of a wall of dry cure cod. Salt cod was a major export from Aberdeen to Europe and South America.

Opposite below: Real Aberdeen finnan kilns at the Allan & Dey processors works, 1911. Three women prepare haddock skewered on rods for placing in the kiln to be smoked. The expansive area within the kiln allowed many hundreds of fish to be smoked at one time. Note the canvas below the broad wooden chimney which would be unrolled to seal smoke within the kiln.

Corner of the 'London Cut' department of Allan & Dey fish processors, c.1900. This large
company provided cured fish for the domestic and export markets, with London being a principal
destination for many of their products. Fish trains would leave from near the quaysides within
hours of the catch being landed, bound for the like of Billingsgate Market.

The Allan & Dey fish processors at their Esplanade curing works, *c*.1920. A large system of pulleys operated drying racks that allowed the artificial drying of salt cod indoors. Such facilities were an obvious necessity in Scotland where outdoor drying could not be relied on.

Other local titles published by Tempus

Aberdeen
ALISTAIR BURNETT

Alistair Burnett has collected over 200 images of Aberdeen in days gone by. From the trams in Union Street to the beach in Victorian times, from shop fronts to suburban streets, all manner of images show Aberdeen of old, in the days when life was more peaceful, when the streets were not jammed with cars and Aberdeen was famed for fish rather than oil.
0 7524 1828 9

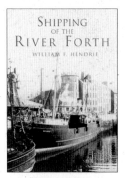

Shipping of the River Forth
WILLIAM F. HENDRIE

For thousands of years the River Forth has been used by man. From Stone Age shell middens to the Roman port at Cramond there is much evidence for man's use of the river and its estuary. From the fishing harbours along the Fife coast to the ports of Grangemouth, Leith and Granton, as well as the naval bases at Rosyth and Port Edgar, the maritime history of the Forth is covered here. Using over 200 illustrations with detailed captions, William F. Hendrie takes us on a tour of the river and its shipping.
0 7524 2117 4

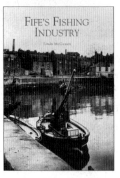

Fife's Fishing Industry
LINDA MCGOWAN

Fishing has always been a mainstay of Fife, a county where nowhere is far from the sea. Linda McGowan charts the growth of the industry through photographs from the archive of the Scottish Fisheries Museum, located in Anstruther. The images concentrate on the East Neuk but other parts of the county are included. The days of hundreds of boats in harbour are long gone but many people in the county still make a living from the sea.
0 7524 2795 4

Herring A History of the Silver Darlings
MIKE SMYLLIE

The story of herring is entwined in the history of commercial fishing. This book looks at the effects of the herring on the people who caught them, their unique ways of life, the superstitions of the fisherfolk, their boats and the communities who lived for the silver darlings. Mike Smyllie lives in Carmarthen and has researched the history of the herring for the past two decades. He has written extensively on fishing vessels and the fishing industry.
0 7524 2988 4

If you are interested in purchasing other books published by Tempus, or in case you have difficulty finding any Tempus books in your local bookshop, you can also place orders directly through our website

www.tempus-publishing.com